Sports Illustrated KIDS

STARS OF SPORTS

NAOMI OSAKA

GRAND SLAM CHAMP

by Cheryl Kim

CAPSTONE PRESS
a capstone imprint

Published by Capstone Editions, an imprint of Capstone
1710 Roe Crest Drive, North Mankato, Minnesota 56003
capstonepub.com

Library of Congress Cataloging-in-Publication Data
Names: Kim, Cheryl, author. Title: Naomi Osaka : grand slam champ / By Cheryl Kim.
Description: North Mankato, Minnesota : Capstone Press, an imprint of Capstone, [2022] | Series: Sports Illustrated kids stars of sports | Includes bibliographical references and index. | Audience: Ages 8-11 | Audience: Grades 4-6 | Summary: "Naomi Osaka is the first Asian tennis player to hold the number one singles ranking in the Women's Tennis Association. She started to make a name for herself at 16 and is now known around the world. Osaka has defeated the toughest players in the league and her talent continues to rise each year. Read more about this skilled tennis star!"—Provided by publisher.
Identifiers: LCCN 2021028239 (print) | LCCN 2021028240 (ebook) | ISBN 9781663983596 (hardcover) | ISBN 9781666323290 (paperback) | ISBN 9781666323306 (pdf) | ISBN 9781666323320 (kindle edition) Subjects: LCSH: Osaka, Naomi, 1997—Juvenile literature. | Women tennis players—Japan—Biography—Juvenile literature. | Women tennis players—United States—Biography—Juvenile literature. | Tennis players—Japan—Biography—Juvenile literature. | Tennis players—United States—Biography—Juvenile literature. Classification: LCC GV994.O73 K56 2022 (print) | LCC GV994.O73 (ebook) | DDC 796.342092 [B]—dc23 LC record available at https://lccn.loc.gov/2021028239 LC ebook record available at https://lccn.loc.gov/2021028240

Editorial Credits
Editor: Christianne Jones; Designer: Bobbie Nuytten; Media Researcher: Morgan Walters; Production Specialist: Laura Manthe

Image Credits
Associated Press: Frank Franklin II, 23, Miami Dolphins, 28; Getty Images: Kyodo News, 7; Newscom: Abaca Press/Dubreuil Corinne, 4, 5, AFP7/ZUMA Press, 21, bareMinerals/MEGA, 26, Haruhiko Otsuka/AFLO, 11, Kyodo, 13, MEGA/Newscom/JMNEW2, 24, Motoo Naka/AFLO, 8, 9; Shutterstock: Chaiwuth Wichitdho, 1, InfantryDavid, 19, Jimmie48 Photography, 15, lev radin, 17, 18, Mai Groves, 12; Sports Illustrated: Erick W. Rasco, Cover, SI Cover, 25

Source Notes
Page 14, "Newcomer of the…," (Cable News Network,) "Naomi Osaka's drive to the top," Cable News Network, http://advertisementfeature.cnn.com, Accessed July 17, 2021.
Page 16, ESPN, "[FULL] 2018 US Open trophy ceremony with Serena Williams and Naomi Osaka |ESPN," YouTube video, 6:18, September 8, 2018, https://www.youtube.com/watch?v=jCm3BemDlj8.
Page 18, ESPN, "[FULL] 2018 US Open trophy ceremony with Serena Williams and Naomi Osaka| ESPN," YouTube video, 7:06, September 8, 2018, https://www.youtube.com/watch?v=jCm3BemDlj8.
Page 19, "Growing up reading…," ESPN News Services, "Naomi Osaka to star in Japanese manga comic book series," November 30, 2020, ESPN, https://www.espn.in, Accessed July 17, 2021.
Page 20, "Mentally it was…," Simon Cambers, "Osaka struggled with 'pressure' of No. 1 ranking," June 29, 2019, ESPN, https://www.espn.com, Accessed July 17, 2021.
Page 20, "I felt like I…," (WION,) "Humbled' Naomi Osaka reveals pressure of being number one," October 7, 2019, WION News, https://www.wionews.com, Accessed July 17, 2021.
Page 20, "I think this dip…," (WION,) "'Humbled' Naomi Osaka reveals pressure of being number one," October 7, 2019, WION News, https://www.wionews.com, Accessed July 17, 2021.
Page 22, "As a kid growing…," Sarah Rendell, "Naomi Osaka lets her latest ad campaign do the talking for Black Lives Matter movement," November 20, 2020, NewsChain, https://www.newschainonline.com, Accessed July 17, 2021.
Page 22, "I'm done being shy…," Christina Macfarlane, "'I have a lot of regrets.' Tennis champion Naomi Osaka opens up about her crippling shyness," June 23, 2020, Cable News Network, https://edition.cnn.com, Accessed July 17, 2021.
Page 22, "Well, what was the…," Sanya Mansoor, "Naomi Osaka says she wore 7 masks about Black Lives during this year's U.S. Open to 'Make people start talking,'" September 13, 2020, Yahoo News, https://news.yahoo.com, Accessed July 17, 2021.
Page 24, "One of the things…," Sydney Clarke, "Naomi Osaka's Braided hairstyle speaks louder than words," November 20, 2020, Refinery29, https://www.refinery29.com, Accessed July 17, 2021.
Page 24, "Huge waves of…," Tumaini Carayol, "Naomi Osaka withdraws from French Open amid row over press conferences," May 31, 2021, The Guardian, https://www.theguardian.com, Accessed July 19, 2021. Page 26, "To me, the…," (PRNewsWire,) "Grand Slam tennis champion, Naomi Osaka, named newest bareMinerals global ambassador," June 20, 2019, PRNewsWire, https://www.prnewswire.com, Accessed July 19, 2021.
Page 27, "One of my main…," (Olympics,) Naomi Osaka: "I hope it's an inspiration to a young girl with big dreams to know that anything is possible," March 8, 2021, Olympics, https://olympics.com, Accessed July 17, 2021.
Page 27, "Aside from tennis…," Liam Hess, "Naomi Osaka is Louis Vuitton's newest brand ambassador," January 11, 2021, Vogue, https://www.vogue.com, Accessed July 18, 2021.
Page 28, "I'm a daughter, a…," Jonathan Jurejko, "Naomi Osaka: How a shy introvert has found her voice to become tennis' new leader," September 14, 2020, BBC Sport, https://www.bbc.com, Accessed July 18, 2021.

All internet sites appearing in back matter were available and accurate when this book was sent to press.

Printed and bound in the United States of America. PO4608

TABLE OF CONTENTS

Words in **BOLD** are in the glossary.

In the final match point in January 2019, Naomi Osaka sent the tennis ball flying straight toward her opponent, Petra Kvitova. Her powerful serve could not be returned. Osaka dropped to the ground as the crowd erupted in cheers. She had come from behind to win her second Grand Slam title.

Almost four months earlier, Osaka, a newcomer, received boos as she unexpectedly won the 2018 U.S. Open title over crowd favorite Serena Williams. This time, she once again proved she was a champion. Her world ranking soared to number one!

〉〉〉 Excitement overtook Osaka in 2019 after her win at the Australian Open.

⟩⟩⟩ Osaka addressed the crowd after her win at Melbourne Park in Australia in 2019.

FACT

The four **annual** Grand Slam tournaments (Australian Open, French Open, Wimbledon, and U.S. Open) are the world's biggest tennis events where players receive the most ranking points, prize money, and media attention.

CHAPTER ONE

HUMBLE BEGINNINGS

Naomi Osaka was born in Osaka, Japan, on October 16, 1997. Her Japanese mother, Tamaki Osaka, and Haitian father, Leonard Francois, met in Japan as students. At the age of three, Naomi **immigrated** with her parents and four-year-old sister, Mari, to Long Island, New York.

Her dad watched the Williams sisters—Serena and Venus—win their first doubles title in the 1999 French Open. This inspired him to teach his own daughters how to play tennis. Although he hadn't played much, he began to coach them.

When Naomi was nine, her family moved into a southern Florida apartment. With dozens of tennis academies in the area, her father looked for coaches who could help continue training the sisters.

〉〉〉 Osaka's mother (second from right) and father (second from left) made many sacrifices for their daughter.

Knowing the family had little money, coach Bill Adams was the first to work with the sisters. Francois agreed to help with tasks in exchange for the girls joining group lessons. Meanwhile, Tamaki worked an office job to help pay the bills.

After a year with Adams, Naomi and Mari practiced on public courts. They often played for five to six hours a day. Meanwhile, their dad looked for new coaches. Christophe Jean helped train the girls for two years. Francois picked up tennis balls on the court to offset the cost of lessons. Then Patrick Tauma agreed to coach. Like the previous coaches, Tauma saw potential. But the family couldn't afford for the girls to keep taking lessons.

The Osaka Sisters

Naomi and Mari spent most of their childhood playing tennis against each other. Naomi credits her sister for shaping her to be the player she is today. Early in Naomi's career, the sisters played in women's doubles matches together. Mari retired from tennis at the age of 24. The two remain close and continue to support each other on their different career paths.

〉〉〉 In 2019, the Osaka sisters played in a doubles match in Tokyo, Japan.

CHAPTER TWO
TURNING PRO

Osaka took an uncommon path to the pros. Like the Williams sisters, she skipped the International Tennis Federation (ITF) junior circuit. She could have played in the junior circuit Grand Slam but chose not to enter. Instead, Osaka wanted to focus on playng in the ITF and the Women's Tennis Association (WTA). On her fourteenth birthday, Osaka played in her first ITF match. She never won a title but was the runner-up in four separate matches between 2011 and 2014.

Right before her sixteenth birthday, Osaka turned pro. She and her parents made the decision to represent Japan. She joined a WTA tour, playing in her first professional match in Japan. At the Pan Pacific Open in Tokyo, Osaka made it to the second round.

A tennis academy in Fort Lauderdale, Florida, offered Osaka a scholarship. Her family moved into a new apartment overlooking the tennis courts. While training there, Osaka qualified for her first WTA main **draw** at the 2014 Stanford Classic.

Osaka was ranked 406th when she played against 19th-ranked Samantha (Sam) Stosur at the Stanford Classic in July 2014. Osaka unexpectedly defeated Stosur and gained international recognition.

⟩⟩⟩ In October 2015, Osaka won the Rising Stars Invitational in Singapore.

In October of that year, Osaka entered as a **wild card** in the Japan Women's Open. She won a match, which launched her rank to 238.

In 2015, she earned her highest career final at the WTA Hua Hin Championships in Thailand. Osaka finished the year ranked 144.

》》》 Osaka in action during day six of the Hua Hin Championships.

Osaka started the 2016 season qualifying for her first Grand Slam main draw at the Australian Open in January. She beat Elina Svitolina (ranked 21) but lost to Victoria Azarenka (ranked 16) in the third round. After beating Sara Errani (ranked 18) at the Miami Open in March, Osaka broke into the top 100 for the first time.

〉〉〉 Osaka showed great focus during her first-round match at the Australian Open in 2016.

NEWCOMER OF THE YEAR

At 18 years old, Osaka **upset** Dominika Cibulkova (ranked 12) in the 2016 Pan Pacific Open. She was the highest ranking player that Osaka defeated. She got into her first WTA final and into the top 50.

In 2016, the WTA named Osaka "Newcomer of the Year." She went on to compete in the U.S. Open in August, making it to the third round.

In late 2017, Osaka hired coach Sascha Bajin to help her game move forward. She played in the Australian Open in 2018 and made it to the fourth round, defeating two top players along the way. Then in March, Osaka won her first title at the Indian Wells Masters in California, beating two of the top five players in the world. Naomi climbed to number 22 in the rankings!

>>> Determination and hard work
helped Osaka move up in the ranks.

CHAPTER THREE
GRAND SLAM

At the 2018 U.S. Open final in September in New York, Osaka played against her childhood **inspiration**, Serena Williams. During the match, Williams received a point violation for throwing her racket down in frustration. After Williams argued with the umpire, he awarded a game point to Osaka. Osaka now led 5–3 with her turn to serve.

On match point, Osaka swatted the tennis ball toward Williams, who hit the ball out of bounds. Osaka had won her first Grand Slam! Disappointed with the results, the crowd booed her at the award ceremony. Osaka pulled her visor down over her tear-filled eyes.

Osaka apologized to the crowd. "I'm sorry it had to end like this. I just want to say thank you for watching the match."

>>> Williams (right) was gracious in defeat as Osaka won the U.S. Open

When asked about the long hug she shared with her mother right after winning, Osaka said, "She sacrificed a lot for me, and it means a lot for her to come and watch my matches. . . . One person I didn't see was my dad because he doesn't physically watch my matches—he walks around, so I'll see him later."

〉〉〉 Osaka celebrates her U.S. Open win with the trophy.

Osaka became the first Japanese player in history to win a Grand Slam tournament. She went on to win her second Grand Slam title in January 2019 at the Australian Open. This time, the crowd cheered loudly for her. Winning consecutive singles titles was a major accomplishment. No other woman had done it since Serena Williams in 2015. The WTA ranked Osaka as the number one player in the world.

Comic Book Star

Osaka is the star in a Japanese manga comic book series. Her sister, Mari, helped produce the comic. "Growing up reading manga/watching anime was something that bonded me and my sister immensely so this is really exciting for both of us." The comic "Unrivaled Naomi Tenka-ichi" is featured in Japan's *Nakayoshi* teen magazine.

STAYING ON TOP

Two weeks after her Australian Open win, Osaka parted ways with coach Bajin. She trained with coach Jermaine Jenkins for six months before returning to work with her father. The pressure of being number one affected Osaka's game. "Mentally it was way more stress and pressure than I could have imagined," she said. "I felt like I shouldn't lose a match after that."

Osaka ended up losing the next three Grand Slams. At the French Open, she lost in the third round. However, she reflected on her losses as being a part of her journey. "I think this dip that I had really humbled me, it made me very motivated to be here right now."

Osaka returned to the U.S. Open in 2020 with Wim Fissette as her coach. She played Victoria Azarenka in the finals. Osaka was a set down but caught up to win the tournament. In 2021, she played in the Australian Open. She beat Serena Williams in the semifinals. Osaka went on to defeat Jennifer Brady and ended up winning her fourth Grand Slam title!

>>> Osaka trains with coach Fissette (left) before the Australian Open.

CHAPTER FOUR
FINDING HER VOICE

During quarantine when **COVID-19** spread around the world, Osaka took time to reflect on her past shyness. "As a kid growing up I never really talked, I was the quiet one."

Since speaking out on social justice issues, she says, "I'm done being shy. I could've shared so many ideas by now, I could've had so many convos . . . but no I'm over here actually putting my own limiter on myself."

At the 2020 U.S. Open, Osaka wore seven different masks for each of the seven rounds she played in. Each mask had the name of a Black person who had lost their life. Her masks brought attention to the **Black Lives Matter** movement and racial **injustice**. When asked what point she was trying to make, Osaka responded, "Well, what was the message that you got? I feel like the point is to make people start talking."

>>> Osaka uses her fame to speak out on issues she cares about, including social justice and mental health issues.

Osaka made headlines for her powerful statement. She also talked about using her tennis **platform**. "One of the things I've learned is that everyone has a platform," she said, "and how they use it is their responsibility."

In 2021, Osaka spoke out about her mental health and how answering questions from reporters caused her "huge waves of anxiety." Osaka decided not to do interviews after her first round win at the French Open. After being fined $15,000 for her missed interview, Naomi withdrew from the tournament.

Osaka shared that she struggled with long periods of depression since her 2018 Grand Slam win and would take time off for self-care. Sponsors and fans supported her decision and admired her courage to bring up important issues on personal health and well-being.

〉〉〉 Osaka was surrounded by press during Media Day at the U.S. Open in 2019.

Sportsperson of the Year

In 2020, *Sports Illustrated* named Osaka Sportsperson of the Year for her athleticism and **activism**. Four others also won the award. Meanwhile, *Time* magazine recognized Osaka as one of the Top 100 Most **Influential** People of the Year.

>>> Osaka posed in bareMinerals makeup for her ad campaign.

Osaka has her share of brand endorsements. The bareMinerals brand chose Osaka as a Power of Good Ambassador in 2019.

"To me, The Power of Good means being the best version of yourself without sacrificing integrity or putting others down," Osaka said.

In 2020, she teamed up with Laureus Sport for Good to create Play Academy with Naomi Osaka. The goal of the academy is to change girls' lives through play and sport.

Osaka said, "One of my main passions away from the court is to support and empower young people around the globe. We're going to be working to ensure more girls stay in sports, building confidence, self-esteem, and leadership skills."

In 2021, Osaka became a brand ambassador and model for fashion designer and icon Louis Vuitton. "Aside from tennis, my most treasured passion is fashion, and there is no brand more iconic than Louis Vuitton," she said.

That same year, Osaka released her first clothing collection with Nike. The fashion line incorporates her Haitian, Japanese, and American heritage.

Naomi Osaka continues to inspire many around the world by embracing who she is and where she came from. "I'm a daughter, a sister, a friend and a girlfriend. I'm Asian, I'm Black, and I'm female. I'm as normal a 22-year-old as anyone, except I happen to be good at tennis. I've accepted myself as just me: Naomi Osaka," she wrote in 2020.

〉〉〉 Osaka waves to fans during the Miami Open in 2021.

TIMELINE

1997 Naomi Osaka is born on October 16 in Osaka, Japan.

2000 Osaka moves to Long Island, New York.

2006 Osaka moves to Florida to enhance her tennis game.

2011 Osaka plays in her first professional qualifying tournament.

2018 Osaka wins her first title at the Indian Wells Masters.

2018 Osaka wins her first Grand Slam title at the U.S. Open.

2019 Osaka wins her second consecutive Grand Slam title at the Australian Open.

2020 Osaka wins her third Grand Slam title at the U.S. Open and makes headlines for wearing seven different customized masks.

2020 Osaka is recognized by *Time* magazine and *Sports Illustrated* for her athleticism and activism.

2021 Osaka wins her fourth Grand Slam title at the Australian Open.

2021 Osaka withdraws from the French Open citing concerns over her mental health.

GLOSSARY

ACTIVISM (AK-ti-viz-um)—actions taken to bring about political or social change

ANNUAL (AN-yew-ul)—happens once a year

BLACK LIVES MATTER (BLAK livz MAT-ur)—a political and social movement protesting violence and racism toward Black people

COVID-19 (KOH-vid nine-TEEN)—a very contagious and sometimes deadly virus that spread worldwide in 2020

DRAW (DRAW)—the schedule of matches in a tennis tournament

IMMIGRATE (IM-mi-grate)—to come into a foreign country to live

INFLUENTIAL (IN-floo-en-shul)—the power to affect others without use of force or commands

INJUSTICE (in-JUS-tis)—disrespecting or harming the rights of another

INSPIRATION (IN-spuh-RAY-shun)—encouraging one's mind and emotions to feel or think in creative ways

PLATFORM (PLAT-form)—media resources a person has to share their ideas

UPSET (UP-set)—when a lower-ranked player defeats a higher-ranked player

WILD CARD (WY-uld KARD)—a player allowed into a tournament even if their ranking isn't high enough

READ MORE

Fishman, Jon M. *Sports All-Stars: Naomi Osaka*. Minneapolis: Lerner Publishing Group, 2021.

Scarbrough, Mary Hertz. *Women in Sports: Naomi Osaka*. Vero Beach, FL: Rourke Educational Media, 2020.

Scheff, Matt. *Naomi Osaka: Biggest Names in Sports*. Minneapolis: Focus Readers, 2020.

INTERNET SITES

Naomi Osaka: Official Site
naomiosaka.com

Olympic Tennis
olympics.com/en/sports/tennis

Tennis Facts for Kids
kids.kiddle.co/Tennis

INDEX

AUTHOR BIO

Cheryl Kim is an elementary teacher from California currently teaching at an international school in Thailand. She lives in Chiang Mai with her husband Brandon and sons Nathanael and Zachary.